IT'S TIME TO LEARN ABOUT ALBATROSS

It's Time to Learn about Albatross

Walter the Educator

Silent King Books
A WhichHead Entertainment Imprint

Copyright © 2025 by Walter the Educator

All rights reserved. No part of this book may be reproduced in any manner whatsoever without written per- mission except in the case of brief quotations embodied in critical articles and reviews.

First Printing, 2024

Disclaimer

This book is a literary work; the story is not about specific persons, locations, situations, and/or circumstances unless mentioned in a historical context. Any resemblance to real persons, locations, situations, and/or circumstances is coincidental. This book is for entertainment and informational purposes only. The author and publisher offer this information without warranties expressed or implied. No matter the grounds, neither the author nor the publisher will be accountable for any losses, injuries, or other damages caused by the reader's use of this book. The use of this book acknowledges an understanding and acceptance of this disclaimer.

It's Time to Learn about Albatross is a collectible early learning book by Walter the Educator suitable for all ages belonging to Walter the Educator's Time to Eat Book Series. Collect more books at WaltertheEducator.com

USE THE EXTRA SPACE TO TAKE NOTES AND DOCUMENT YOUR MEMORIES

ALBATROSS

High above the ocean blue,

It's Time to Learn about
Albatross

A mighty bird comes into view.

With wings so wide and strong and free,

It glides across the endless sea.

The albatross is big and grand,

With feathers white and wings so spanned.

It barely flaps but soars with grace,

Floating high in open space.

Its wings can stretch so long, so wide,

To help it glide with wind as guide.

For days and weeks it sails with ease,

Riding waves and ocean breeze.

It dips and dives to catch its meal,

With fish and squid its beak will steal.

A clever bird that hunts so deep,

Then soars back up with one great leap!

It's Time to Learn about
Albatross

Albatrosses find their way,

Through stormy skies and misty spray.

With eyes so sharp and senses keen,

They spot their home where they have been.

They dance and sing to find a mate,

A partner true, a lifelong fate.

They tap their beaks, they spread their wings,

They bow and twist, such lovely things!

Their eggs rest safe upon the ground,

In nests where both parents are found.

They take turns warm and keeping tight,

Until the chick is full of might.

But dangers lurk in ocean deep,

With plastic trash and nets that sweep.

Their food grows scarce, their paths unclear,

It's Time to Learn about

Albatross

They need our help to calm their fear.

By keeping oceans clean and bright,

We help these birds stay strong in flight.

Protect their home, protect their space,

So they can soar with speed and grace.

So if you see one flying high,

Like a shadow in the sky,

Remember how it roams so free,

It's Time to Learn about

Albatross

The albatross, king of the sea!

ABOUT THE CREATOR

Walter the Educator is one of the pseudonyms for Walter Anderson. Formally educated in Chemistry, Business, and Education, he is an educator, an author, a diverse entrepreneur, and he is the son of a disabled war veteran.
"Walter the Educator" shares his time between educating and creating. He holds interests and owns several creative projects that entertain, enlighten, enhance, and educate, hoping to inspire and motivate you. Follow, find new works, and stay up to date with Walter the Educator™

at WaltertheEducator.com

www.ingramcontent.com/pod-product-compliance
Lightning Source LLC
LaVergne TN
LVHW052016060526
838201LV00059B/4056